Cowboy Puzzles

Stella Maidment and Daniela Dogliani

QED

QED Publishing

Editor: Alexandra Koken
Designer: Elaine Wilkinson

Copyright © QED Publishing 2012

First published in the UK in 2012 by
QED Publishing
A Quarto Group company
230 City Road
London EC1V 2TT

www.qed-publishing.co.uk

A catalogue record for this book is available from the British Library.

ISBN 978 1 84835 862 1

Printed in China

If you get stuck,
the answers are
at the back of
the book!

Howdy!
Welcome to the Wild West!

This is Rocky the cowboy.

And this is his horse, Grace.

Solve the puzzles in this book and help Rocky find the stolen money bags.

Look out for Bob the dog too. You'll find him in every picture!

Rocky and Grace are on their way to town.

Which way should they go?

Can you spot these things?

a wagon wheel

a bird

two white cows

4

BANK

SALOON

PONY EXPRESS

SHERIFF

GENERAL STORE

HARDWARE

Rocky ties Grace up
outside the store.

GENERAL
STORE

6

Can you find four differences between Grace and the other horse?

HARDWARE

Can you spot these things?

a rocking chair

a black cat

three horseshoes

Today, Rocky is buying a new pair of cowboy boots.

Can you match the pairs?

Can you spot
these things?

a jar of sweets

a pumpkin

two saucepans

9

Outside the store, everyone is looking at a poster.

WANTED

BAD BILL
FOR STEALING MONEY
FROM THE BANK

Can you see the sheriff? He's wearing a gold star.

Can you spot these things?

a baby cowboy

a doll

two blue and white shirts

BANK

11

Rocky decides to find Bad Bill.
"Which way did he go?" asks Rocky.

"Towards the Red Mountains," says the sheriff.
Which path should Rocky and Grace take?

Can you spot
these things?

three
black birds
a wagon

a wolf

13

"Oh no! There are huge rocks blocking our path," cries Rocky.

Can you spot these things?

two snakes

two trees

a bear

14

Can you help them find a safe path across the canyon?

That night, Rocky and Grace
camp under the stars.

Can you spot
these things?

a red and black blanket

a can of beans

two mice

The stars form shapes in the sky.
Can you see what they are?

Next morning, Rocky finds different kinds of footprints in the sand.

Can you spot these things?

three yellow flowers

a lizard

a rabbit

18

Follow the horseshoe trail and see where it goes.

RODEO

Bad Bill is at the rodeo!

He has a black hat and a moustache.
Can you find him?

Can you spot these things?

two blue boots

a black and white horse

a green waistcoat

21

When the cowboys throw their lassos, Rocky joins in.

Who catches Bad Bill?

Can you spot these things?

a red hat

a black saddle

three money bags

23

Rocky brings Bad Bill and the bank's money safely back to town.

Can you find the twins in the crowd?

Can you spot these things?
two guitars

a white dog

a doll

24

25

The sheriff is so pleased he makes Rocky his deputy!

He also has four apples as treats for Grace.
Can you find them?

Can you spot
these things?

a silver deputy's
badge

handcuffs

Bob's bone

Answers

Pages 4-5

Bob

Follow the red line to town.

Pages 6-7

Bob

The four differences are circled in red.

Pages 8-9

Bob

The red lines show which boots match.

Pages 10-11

Bob

The sheriff is circled in red.

28

Pages 12-13

The path in the centre leads to the
Red Mountains.

Pages 14-15

Follow the red line across the canyon.

Pages 16-17

The shapes in the sky are: a boot, a cow, a cat,
a horse, a horseshoe and a cowboy hat.

Pages 18-19

The horseshoe trail goes to the rodeo!

29

Answers

Pages 20-21

Bad Bill is circled in red.

Pages 22-23

Rocky catches Bad Bill!

Pages 24-25

Bob

The twins are circled in red.

Pages 26-27

Bob

The apples for Grace
are circled in red.

More cowboy fun

Cowboy day
Dress up as a cowboy for the day. Wear a checked shirt, a cowboy hat and make a cardboard sheriff's star. Maybe you could even host a cowboy-themed party!

Memory game
Cut out 12 same-sized pieces of card or paper. Make pairs by drawing the same items on two cards. For example, two cowboy boots or two lassos. Mix the cards up and lay them on a table face down. Turn over two cards at a time until you find a pair. Carry on until you've matched them all up!

Catch that thief!
Just as Rocky finds Bad Bill, you and a friend can be cowboys searching for your own baddie. Choose a cuddly toy to be the 'thief' and take turns to hide it somewhere in your home. The person who is being the cowboy has to try to find where the thief is hiding. Help the cowboy by saying "You're getting warm" as he gets closer to the toy and "You're getting cold" as he gets further away.

Pin the tail on the horse
Draw a horse on a large piece of paper, leaving out the tail. Then make a tail out of a strip of paper. Stick the horse picture to the wall. Add some sticky tack to the top of the tail and see if you can stick it in the right place without looking!